GOING MOBILE

LIBERTY UNDER ATTACK PUBLICATIONS

Copyleft Notice

This book is covered by a BipCot NoGovernment License. Re-use and modification is permitted to anyone EXCEPT for governments and the bludgies thereof.

Further Use Permission: Please feel free to use, re-use, distribute, copy, re-print, take credit for, steal, broadcast, mock, hate, quote, misquote, or modify this book in any way you see fit. Sell it, make copies and hand it out at concerts, make t-shirts, print it on flying disks, or do anything else because intellectual property is a State based haven of the weak, the stupid, and those lacking confidence in their own ability.

# LIBERTY UNDER ATTACK PUBLICATIONS *tell your story*

Looking for your next read or listen?

1. **Adventures in Illinois Law: Witnessing Tyranny Firsthand** by Shane Radliff (Audiobook/Anthology)
2. **Adventures in Illinois Higher Education: Communist Indoctrination** by Shane Radliff (Audiobook/Anthology)
3. **An Illusive Phantom of Hope: A Critique of Reformism** by Kyle Rearden (Audiobook/Anthology)
4. **The Production of Security** by Gustave de Molinari (Audiobook)
5. **Are Cops Constitutional?** by Roger Roots (Audiobook)
6. **Vonu: The Search for Personal Freedom** by Rayo (Audiobook)
7. **Argumentation Ethics: An Anthology** by Hans-Herman Hoppe et al (Anthology)
8. **Just Below The Surface: A Guide to Security Culture** by Kyle Rearden (Audiobook/Anthology)
9. **Sedition, Subversion, and Sabotage, Field Manual No. 1: A Three Part Solution to the State** by Ben Stone (Audiobook)
10. **#agora** by anonymous (Paperback and Kindle)
11. **Vonu: A Strategy for Self-Liberation** by Shane Radliff (Paperback/Audiobook)
12. **Second Realm: Book on Strategy** by Smuggler and XYZ (Paperback)
13. **Vonu: The Search for Personal Freedom** by Rayo (Special Paperback Reprint/Audiobook)
14. **Vonu: The Search for Personal Freedom, Part 2 [Letters From Rayo]** (Paperback)
15. **Going Mobile** by Tom Marshall (Paperback/Audiobook)
16. **Anarchist to Abolitionist: A Bad Quaker's Journey** by Ben Stone
17. **Brushfire, A Thriller** by Matthew Wojtecki

Looking for a publisher? Drop us a line:
WWW.LIBERTYUNDERATTACK.COM

TRANSCRIBER'S FOREWORD

As I've mentioned before, my preferred vonu strategy has always been to find my freedom on the open ocean. That goal remains the same, yet there is another option available that could come into fruition sooner, inexpensively, and with little additional experience necessary—that option being van nomadism.

This is the strategy Rayo started with before he pursued wilderness vonu—he got sick of the "talkers" and the lack of "doers," and decided to move out of his apartment into a camper mounted on a pickup truck.

That was the beginning of his vonu journey—it very well might be mine, too.

Nonetheless, the publication you are about to read is *Going Mobile*; it appears this is another one put together by Jim Stumm. Rayo (or, as he is referred to in the publication, "Tom, from Preform") contributed a number of articles and we find out that he even gave a public talk on the subject of van nomadism in 1968, which seems odd considering some of the things he has written about in the past.

If you are even a tad bit interested in pursuing van nomadism, this publication is *almost* all you will need. Herein, you will learn about: a handful of vonuans' experiences pursuing this strategy, considerations regarding the purchase of vans, buses, and campers, converting your vehicle for living aboard, how to choose the best "squat spot", and electricity/comfort in your automobile, among other things.

Keep in mind, most of these articles/notes/letters were written from the late 1960s to the mid-1980s. Some of the information may be outdated.

A couple quick technical notes before turning you over to the publication: first off, I made an "executive" decision to move the "Note from Hal S." after "Auto Living – In A Pinch," in order to keep the letters/notes together making up an entire chapter.

Secondly, I have added some images of vans, campers, buses, etc. that are mentioned in the following articles, for formatting purposes and to provide you, the reader, with an idea of what the authors are referencing.

How important is freedom (or, invulnerability to coercion) to you? Are you willing to change your lifestyle in pursuance of it? If so, there is no simpler, inexpensive, and more practical strategy than van nomadism.

Shane Radliff
September 2017
Liberty Under Attack & *The Vonu Podcast*

GO "GYPSY" – NOW! (Oct. 1968)
By: Tom Marshall (Rayo)

Now is the time when the tied people return from their summertime escapist rituals & put themselves away in their boxes for another year. And now is the time for free people to look for bargains in vans & campers.

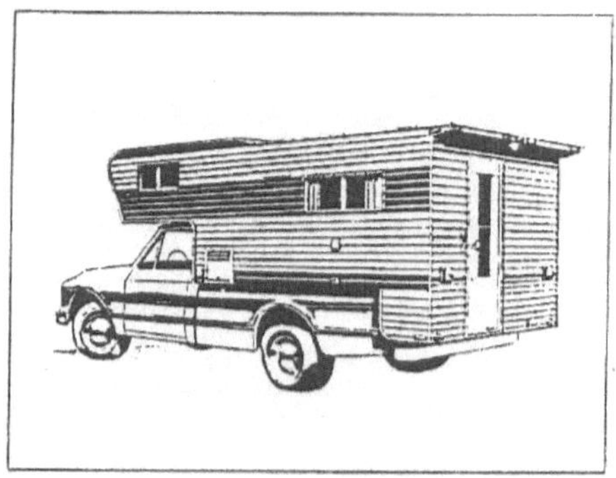

Do you hesitate for lack of funds? Nomadic living is THE least expensive way of living that still allows easy access to the city. There is no rent to pay. If 5 to 10 grand for a new rig is more than you can afford, look for used wheels. I saw a well-equipped bread truck offered for $900.

Do you hesitate for lack of knowledge? Unlike setting off on a yacht for the south seas or building your own log cabin in Northern Canada, land-mobile living requires few skills you don't already have. A truck is no more difficult to drive than an automobile; some even have automatic transmission. If you don't know your way around the innards, by all means contract with a mechanically-proficient friend to do the shopping, making sure he understands YOUR needs.

Do you dislike the thought of "always travelling?" Strange as it might seem, a nomad probably moves very little. Travelling is what the guy does who buys a house to "settle down," & then commutes to work – back & forth & back and forth & back & forth...

Are you awaiting a nomadic intentional community to move into, & with? Why let YOUR liberation wait on OTHERS? If it is companionship you want, become a nomad; you can associate even with stationary dwellers easier than can another stationary dweller; you can pick & change your neighbors at will.

Do you wonder how you will live when you are free? With some thought & experimentation you can develop a life pattern that is efficient & satisfying for you.

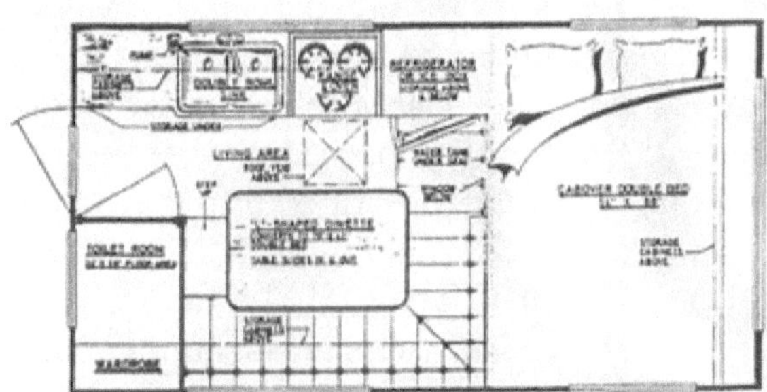

SELF-LIBERATION SEMINAR (June 1968)
By: Tom Marshall (Rayo)

I was a participant in Atlantis Enterprise's "Self Liberation" seminar held in Los Angeles this May. Five patterns of living for realizing personal freedom in the here-and-now were described & compared as to cost, freedom & safety for a "model" family of 2 adults & 3 children. These were: clandestine urban, underground shelter, remote homestead, land-mobile nomadic, & sea-mobile nomadic. The model land-mobile family was described thusly in the seminar notes:

> The <u>LAND-MOBILE NOMAD</u> family lives in 2 campers. They have scouted & prepared a number of "squat-spots" at different locations but all on uninhabited non-privately-owned land. The family as a whole moves from squat-spot to squat-spot; the pattern of movement is somewhat seasonal. When funds are needed, one parent commutes weekly to the city utilizing the smaller camper for transportation & city housing. The other parent & children live in the larger camper which remains at the squat-spot, which is where the children are educated. For auxiliary storage they have caches & rented space outside the city. They do some foraging but, partly because of easy proximity of city work & stores, rely mainly on purchased supplies. Protection is through concealment while at the squat-sport, mobility when disturbed, & anonymity while traveling in the city.

I presented the land-mobility topic. Tracing the historical development of stationary residence, I hypothesized that the "industrialization" of agriculture had made obsolete attached dwellings for most of the population. I described the advantages of nomadic living & suggested ways to overcome the significant disadvantage: limited space. For the "model" family I recommended 2 self-propelled vehicles over camper plus trailer, camper plus tent, or single large vehicle. However the camper-plus-tent combination costs the least. For wilderness living I recommended selection & preparation of secret "squat-spots" rather than reliance on supervised campgrounds in National Forests. Suggestions for finding "squat-spots": Explore especially gently-rolling wooded land that has been logged; trees provide concealment & shade; water sources likely; a profusion of old logging trails can be easily improved.

In comparison with the other "self-liberational" modes as well as 3 "conventional" modes (urban rental, urban ownership, rural ownership), land-mobility rated lowest in overall cost in those situations requiring city employment. For present freedom & future safety, land-mobility is generally rated 2nd only to sea-mobility which is much more expensive.

LETTER FROM A NOMAD (1969)
By: Tom (of Preform)

I've been nomadic more than a year so most of the novelty has worn off, it seems natural. I recall several phases: inundated with the work of getting moved into the camper (plus some rented storage space); fear of unknown (will I be able to find places to park where I won't be harassed?); joy of liberation, almost like a perpetual vacation, celebration, FREEDOM; growing in freedom, growth pains (what do I do now?); press of mundane responsibilities that become part of a way of life, should tune up the engine, ought to put out another issue of PREFORM.

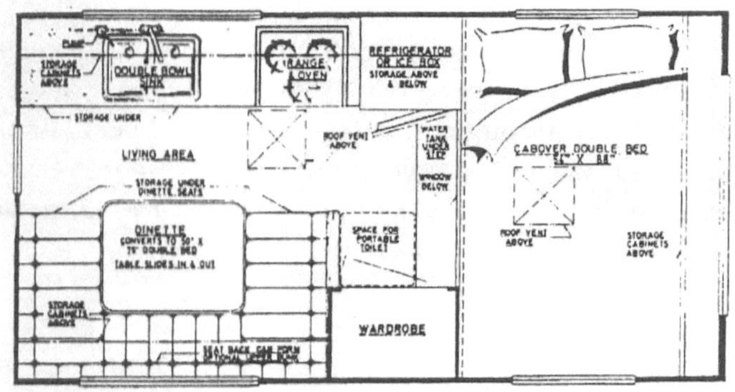

The only psychological problem I have so far identified is one not unique to nomadic living but encountered, I suspect, by almost every opt out, regardless of lifestyle: most of his life has been structured by other people & events; he has been told what to do & when to do it. Now, suddenly, he is largely free of all this. His life is all his to structure as he will. And this is a responsibility which overwhelms many people. I think this partly explains those who are loudly critical of the society around them, but firmly rooted, & who if propositioned will have no end of objections to ANY here & now self liberation approach. Do they subconsciously sense their psychological dependency on some of the things they say they hate, & dread the thought of full responsibility for their own lives, no one else to blame for their shortcomings?

Perhaps "xenophobic rejection" of nomadic life stems not from its strangeness but from its accessibility: almost anyone CAN become substantially free this way, easily, inexpensively, through their own effort, any time they choose. It's an onus upon the exclusively armchair philosophers to "put up or shut up," since they are not about to do either, they angrily reject any consideration of it. On the other hand, they will happily speculate about a Free America (or world) of the next millennium because it is safely distant, puts upon them no self responsibility to act.

Back to the problem's personal manifestations: I still have nagging doubts about not accomplishing as much as I like as soon as I think I should. For example, some time ago I decided I should become a crack offhand shot with 22 rifle, & relearn to shoot left handed to use my better eye. I resolved to practice dry fire twice a day. But I haven't stuck to it. A Monday to Friday (plus overtime on Saturday) net builder would have all kinds of excuses to himself. But I haven't a one. I know I could set up some kind of artificial time allocation system for myself, completely with goody points & baddy points, but so far I have always hesitated thinking that there is a more natural way I will grow into, instead of creating my own personal boss surrogate. The tasks to which come off best are those which lend themselves to concentrated effort: I have been working on PREFORM, full time, 12 to 14 hours a day, for nearly 2 days now (amazing how much time one of these little sheets can consume) & will probably continue until I finish, then do almost nothing on it for several months until I put out the next issue.

I find I avoid cognitive dissonance more & more by cutting off dissonant communication: almost never read Establishment publications, rarely listen to the radio, & have no social relations with non libertarians. On a job (consultant, part time) I limit communication to matters concerning work. I avoid most of the little day to day petty irritations of the Servile Society which are probably as important in psychological paralyzation [sic] as the big scary stuff.

I have developed my living patterns to the point where 2/3rds of my time is spent parked "in the hills" only 1/3 in the city. Right now, however (when I answered the letter), I am in a shopping center parking lot in Santa Monica, sorting out mail I just picked up, feasting on ground chuck & sherbet, which I can't store or gather in the wilderness. I was focused on correspondence until I introspected just now in response to this letter; I was rather oblivious to environment. I wonder if other shoppers passing the camper can hear the typewriter?

If so, what might they think? (I doubt they hear it above the background noise; however I don't type late at night when in the city.)

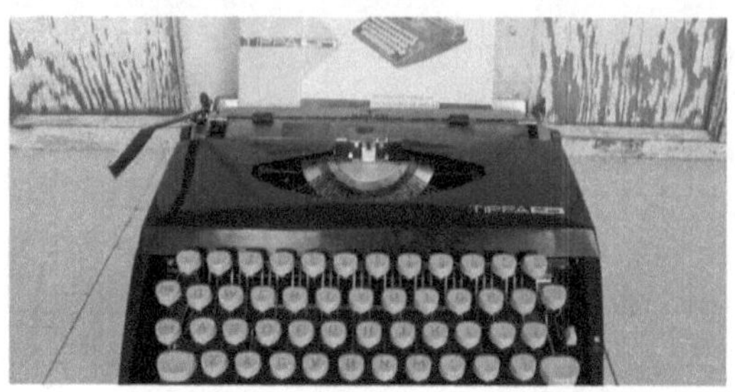

    (While publishing this issue of PREFORM, on the other hand, I'm at a squat spot along Coast Highway. It's on the side of a hill, old homesite, I believe; remains of a water tank with a pipe out of the hill, still flowing. Perhaps the people were forced out & the land taken by the govt, which has something not far away. It's been used a few times as a dump. It's less than a quarter mile from the ocean & highway; I can hear surf & traffic. Concealment seems marginal; the roof of my camper might be visible from a short stretch of the highway & at night I can see distant lights (Port Hueneme?), but I haven't been molested. I've been here total of 2 weeks on 2 occasions. Something which helps: the trail to the site is rather steep for the average auto; my rig has 35:1 low gear ratio & 2/3 of the weight on rear wheels. I bought some meat & fresh fruit when passing through Ojai several days ago, but that is all gone so I am back to staples, wild greens, & vitamin C. Wild mustard grows here, prolific with all the rain, I had a potful for dinner.)

ABOUT "PREFORM" (Sept. 1969)
By: Tom & Roberta

We – PREFORM'S editors – live in a truck camper, "squatting" most of the time in uninhabited mountain regions of California. (As we are learning, this is only one of many neo-nomadic life-styles). Since we avoid rent, eat what we forage plus bulk-purchased staples, & (most important) stay out of status games, expenses are very low. What little money we need comes from part-time jobs as independent contractors (no taxes withheld) in Los Angeles. When working, one of us commutes weekly & sleeps while in the city in a small station wagon. For recreation we have the outdoors plus intellectual pursuits. We travel relatively little – far less than does the conventional city dweller commuting between work & his little box. But what traveling we do is enjoyable: we spent 2 months last summer in a wilderness area of British Columbia. While we find individual nomadism more than satisfactory we also look forward to compatible associations & (perhaps) to evolvement of one or more libertarian-nomadic intentional communities. PREFORM is typed & mimeoed "on board"; mail & messages are received through a friend.

"Stop asking me if we're almost there!
We're *nomads*, for crying out loud!"

THE NOMADS (WALL STREET JOURNAL, Aug. 21, 1978)
By: Douglas R. Sease

<u>TO THOUSANDS IN U.S., HOME, SWEET HOME IS A PLACE WITH WHEELS: And the Place Can Be Tiny Or Positively Luxurious; A Bunch of Freeloaders?</u>

Three Years Ago, Alfred Sevilla's house in Paducah, KY, burned to the ground. He tried renting, but landlords were reluctant to rent to a family of six. When Mr. [Sevilla] did find a willing landlord with a large-enough house, the rent he had to pay was nearly prohibitive on a truck driver's salary.

So, after the house was sold earlier this year, Mr. Sevilla paid $1100 for a used 8-by-11-foot camper for the back of his pickup truck, loaded his family & a friend into his 2 cars, & left Kentucky for a new home & a new job.

Today the Sevillas are living near the Gulf of Mexico – they don't want their location given for fear that problems they left in Kentucky will catch up with them – & all seven persons are living in their tiny camper. Despite the crowded quarters, there are advantages. Rent amounts to only $150 a month, including utilities, & the kids have access to fishing, nearby beaches, a swimming pool & a recreation room. In fact, the Sevillas are finding their new way of life so attractive that they don't plan to ever settle down again.

"I'll never own another house as long as I live," the 38-year-old Mr. Sevilla says. "If you own a house, you're a slave to it, & we want our freedom."

Modern Gypsies

The Sevillas are among untold thousands of people who, for a variety of reasons, have chosen to become nomads. These modern Gypsies have no permanent home, preferring instead to live & roam in vehicles ranging from small campers to luxurious motor homes, which they park in places ranging from commercial camping facilities with swimming pools & game rooms to shopping center parking lots & country roads.

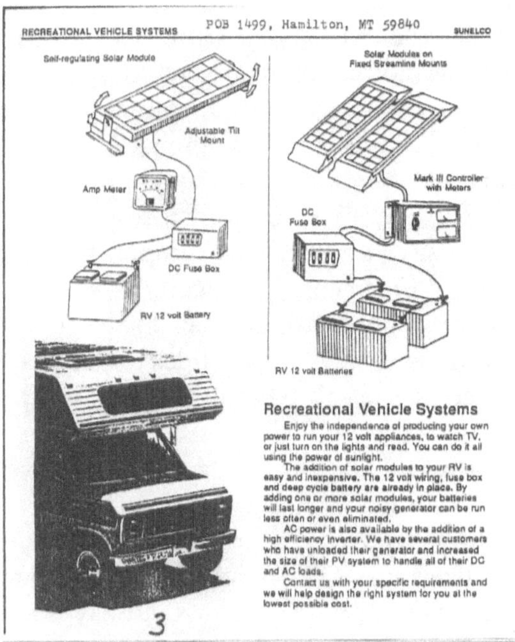

Recreational Vehicle Systems

Enjoy the independence of producing your own power to run your 12 volt appliances, to watch TV, or just turn on the lights and read. You can do it all using the power of sunlight.

The addition of solar modules to your RV is easy and inexpensive. The 12 volt wiring, fuse box and deep cycle battery are already in place. By adding one or more solar modules, your batteries will last longer and your noisy generator can be run less often or even eliminated.

AC power is also available by the addition of a high efficiency inverter. We have several customers who have unloaded their generator and increased the size of their PV system to handle all of their DC and AC loads.

Contact us with your specific requirements and we will help design the right system for you at the lowest possible cost.

Many of these people are retirees, trying to stretch meager pensions or intent on seeing the world. Others are pursuing their line of work, & a small number are running from something. But whatever the reason, these people don't have any roots & don't want any.

"If we find out we don't like this place or the people, we can pick up & go anytime we want, "Mr. Sevilla says. "We don't have to worry about getting some sucker to buy a house that's falling apart."

No one knows how many nomads there are. Measuring such a mobile population would be difficult, & the Census Bureau doubts that the group is very large.

"I, for one, don't believe that there's a great migration into these tin lizzies," says William Downs of the bureau's housing division. However, Mr. Downs acknowledges that the bureau will attempt to measure these transients in the 1980 census, & campground operators, recreational-vehicle salesmen & the nomads themselves think the bureau may be surprised. "There aren't exact figures," says Wayne Frederick, executive director of the Florida Campground Association, "but I guarantee you this is a very big & increasing thing.

Reservations Recommended

"You ought to see this place around November," says a recreational-vehicle salesman in Sarasota, FL. "The highway will be jammed with people coming down here to spend the winter in the campgrounds." Many campground operators in South Florida warn that anyone without a reservation in August for a winter campsite will find pickings slim.

Richard G. RuBino, an associate professor of urban planning at Florida State University & a part-time camper, has seen enough people living on the road to become concerned about their impact on government services. He warned that local governments may be overwhelmed eventually by shifting tides of migrants who demand government services but don't pay the property taxes to support those services.

"Think of the problems for the school system if a road-construction crew comes into a small town & settles temporarily," warns Prof. RuBino, who is preparing an informal survey of Florida campgrounds to determine what percentage of the campers live in their vehicles full time. "The school system would have to be able to service a population at its peak."

One of the Motives

Some people do take to the road to escape property taxes. "I'll pay my federal tax because I have to," says a full-time camper who is staying near Mobile, Ala., "but I'll never pay a property tax again. I'm not about to support some idiot tax assessor who comes around every year & tells me I owe more taxes. To hell with that."

Yet many modern nomads resent the notion that they are freeloading.

"We pay our rent to the campground, & the campground owner pays his taxes," says a camper in a park near Valdosta, GA. "Besides," he says, "we spend a lot of money in local stores."

Many local officials around the country agree that full-time campers pay their own way. "They don't cost us much in the way of services, & they're great for the local economy," says Hugh H. Riley, tax assessor for Cameron County, Texas, a popular wintering spot for the road people. "We've got our doors open to them."

Not everyone is so hospitable. Matthew Sugarman, head ranger at Point Mugu State Park near Ventura, Calif., suspects that road people who don't want to pay the park's overnight camping fees are responsible for much of the pilferage & vandalism in his park. Some brazenly drive their vehicles into the park after the gatekeeper has left. They then use the park's facilities, including dumping tanks into which the vehicles' sewage holding tanks are emptied, & leave before the gatekeeper returns the next morning.

"They're just freeloading off the state," Mr. Sugarman complains.

In Copiah County, Miss., county supervisors recently hired a caretaker & deputized him after several construction workers & their families set up housekeeping in the Georgetown Water Park, a county-maintained riverside facility offering free camping for short stays only.

"We don't mind folks coming to visit with us for a few days," says Lawnrence Hood, Copiah County chancery clerk, "but freeloading off us is another matter. We told them to move on. And since the caretaker could have taken them to jail, they didn't argue."

Most full-time campers aren't trying to get by on the sly, but many are trying to stretch retirement incomes. If they plan well, life on the road can be very inexpensive.

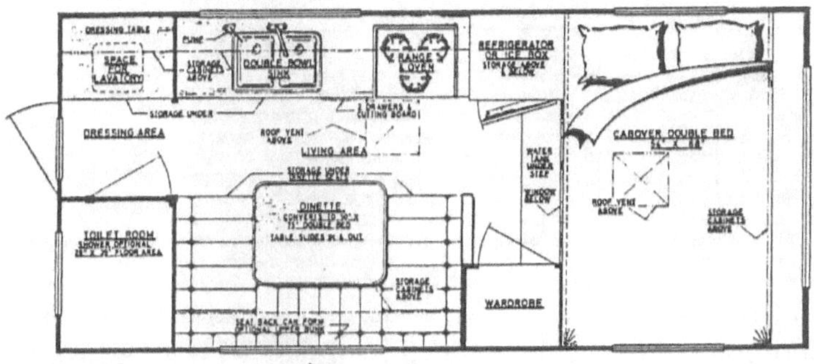

Until six years ago, Fred & Joy Kilburn ran their own insurance & real-estate business in Hoodsport, Wash. Today the Kilburns — he is 67 years old & she is 65 — have a total monthly income of about $700. They figure that the cost of living in the battered old 21-foot Airstream trailer is only about $400 a month. While seeking cool mountain breezes in the summer & the warm weather of Florida in the winter, the Kilburns have built up a sizable savings account.

The cramped quarter common to the smaller travel trailers & motor homes don't bother the people who live in them. Most prefer to remain outdoors as much as possible. But carefully organized interiors make living indoors in bad weather tolerable.

The Kilburns have some photographs of their daughters on tiny shelves in their trailers, but there are few knickknacks. Clothes, dishes, & utensils are in limited supply too. And the Kilburns use local libraries rather than buy their own books.

"You don't need all those other things," Mrs. Kilburn says. "I know a lot of women who don't think they could live without a sewing room, but I just don't need all that space."

The lack of privacy can be a problem in smaller vehicles, especially for large families. While Mr. Sevilla asserts that "privacy is just a state of mind," he & his wife acknowledge that their sex life has been "practically nonexistent" since the family moved into the camper. Mr. Sevilla plans to buy a second, larger trailer so that the family can get some privacy. The second trailer, he says, also will give the children a place to study during the school year.

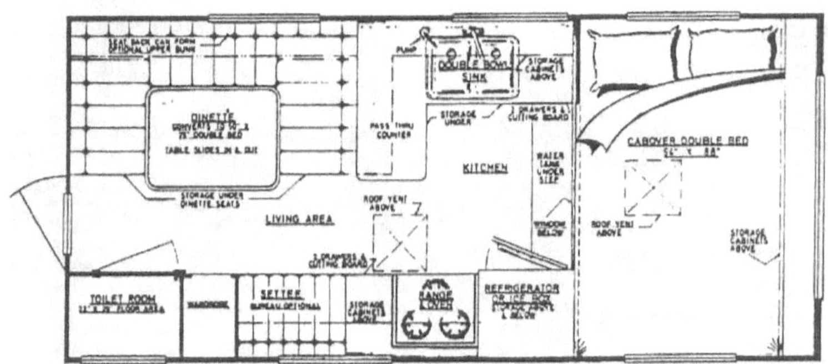

For anyone who wants to avoid close quarters, the price of full-time camping rises quickly. A 30-foot trailer with a bathroom, kitchen & small bedroom can run well over $10,000, & the cost of a powerful truck or car to pull it must be considered, too. Similarly, a 30-foot self-propelled motor coach can cost $50,000 &, unless the occupants are willing to unhook from water, electrical & sewer lines every time they want to go to the store, they must also own a car.

Depreciation is another expensive factor for the larger vehicles. Unlike most homes, a recreational vehicle loses value over the years, sometimes quite sharply. Repairs are also more frequent -- & sometimes more costly – than they would be in a house.

But the extra expense can buy such luxuries as two, or even three, air conditioners, a built-in vacuum-cleaner system, a color television set, a refrigerator-freezer, a microwave oven & a stereo sound system.

Full-sized tubs are usually standard features in bathrooms, & the bedrooms usually can easily accommodate a queen-sized bed.

For people like David Henry, a 49-year-old travelling representative for Kirsch Co. of Sturgis Mich., a drapery-equipment manufacturer, such luxuries make living on the road an attractive alternative to commuting between a house & a sales territory.

Mr. Henry visits architects in 60 cities around the Southeast in his 31-foot motor coach, towing an American Motors Corp. Gremlin. When he comes to a new city, he either finds a campsite or simply pulls into a half-empty shopping-center parking lot. Within minutes he can be in the Gremlin making his first calls. At day's end Mr. Henry returns to the motor home & cooks dinner, then relaxes in one of the comfortable armchairs to watch television or read.

In His Own Bed

"The most attractive thing about this kind of life is that I can spend each night in my own bed," Mr. Henry says. He has also found that he doesn't have to worry about airline reservations, car rentals or motel accommodations, so he can devote more time to his job.

He figures he is saving Kirsch Co. some money. ""When I first proposed this three years ago, the company said, 'Hell, no, we don't want any damn gypsies representing the company,'" Mr. Henry recalls, but after he showed that he could save an estimated $2000 a year on airline tickets & car rentals, "they said go ahead." He has been on the road ever since & is preparing to buy an even larger motor home soon.

The logistics of living on the road aren't too complicated. Most full-time campers, after an initial burst of cross-country travel, restrict their wanderings to a favorite section of the country, where they rent a post office box or have their mail delivered to a relative. Mr. Henry uses the Kirsch Co. regional headquarters in Atlanta, where he has even rigged up an electrical connection for his motor home behind the company's warehouse.

A Pay Phone and a Grocery

Most campgrounds have a pay telephone, which is all most campers say they want or need — "you think we want a phone after having our own business for all those years?" says Mrs. Kilburn — as well as a small grocery store where staples can be purchased.

Credit cards are crucial on the road, since most merchants won't accept out-of-town checks. Driver's licenses & registrations are obtained in those states in which the occupants spend the most time. Not surprisingly, few full-time campers vote, mostly because they aren't in one place long enough to become involved in local issues or to meet residency requirements. Medical help is only as far away as the nearest hospital.

One of the advantages of life on the road is that a person can seek out the best possible services. Mr. Henry, for instance, goes to a mechanic in once city for front-end work on his motor home, & to a mechanic in another city for engine work. And when he recently found that he needed a gall bladder operation, he drove to the Duke University Medical Center at Durham, N.C., because he heard he could get the best care there. When his hospital roommate began hallucinating one night, Mr. Henry checked out, spent the night in his motor room in the emergency-room parking lot, & then checked back in the next morning.

Sources:
1) <u>SUNELCO</u>, the sun electric company (POB 1499, Hamilton, MT 59840). Solar panels, batteries, lights, etc. Planning guide & catalog: $3.95.
2) <u>Real Goods</u> (966 Mazzoni St, Ukiah, CA 95482). World's largest selection of offline power equipment: solar systems & components, 12 volt appliances, lights, etc. "Alternative Energy Sourcebook," 400 pages, $14, refundable with $100 order, or request <u>free</u> catalog.
3) <u>Car Books</u> (175 Hudson St, Hackensack, NJ 07601. Shop manuals for every make of truck, van, & car, & a few RV books like: "Customizing Your Van" & "RV Owners Manual." Catalog $2.00.
4) <u>J.C. Whitney</u> (POB 8410, Chicago, IL 60680). Huge catalog of truck, van, & car parts & accessories, with a dozen pages of parts for RVs, vans, campers, etc. Catalog $2.00.
5) <u>HOME POWER</u> (POB 130, Hornbrook CA 96044). <u>Free</u> magazine, mostly covers stationary independent power systems for remote cabins & homesteads, but also provides much info on solar panels, batteries, inverters, generators, & 12 volt equipment that is relevant to RVs.
6) <u>INNOVATOR, Mar/Apr 68</u> – issue of n/1 [?] about land mobility & "retreat" (survivalism). Contents include: letter from a nomad (describes his way of life); buying a mobile home (types, size, running

gear, materials, furnishings, purchase, registration); do-it-yourself van; location & shelter (where to retreat, region, homesite, retreat home); mobility, an alternate retreat concept; & more. 10 pages, order #MA68, $1.25 postpaid, order from: Jim Stumm, Box 29, Hiler Branch, Buffalo, NY 14223.

7) <u>Escapees Club</u> (Rt. 5, Box 310, Livingston, TX 77351). Clubs for nomads provides address for mail & phone answering service, some free campsites, & 6 newsletters a year.

8) <u>Fredson RV Supply</u> (815 North Harbor Blvd, Santa Ana, CA 92703). Huge selection of RV & 12 volt equipment. Catalog $3.00.

9) <u>Woodall's Campground Directory</u> (Woodall Publishing Co, 11 North Skokie Highway, Suite 205, Lake Bluff, IL 60044). Huge directory of campsites in USA, Canada, & Mexico, with maps & descriptions, updated annually. Price $14.30 postpaid.

10) <u>Don Wright's Guide to Free Campgrounds</u> (Lifestyle Publications, 24396 Pleasant View Drive, Elkhart, IN 46517). Identifies 6000 campsites, listed by state. Price $14.95 postpaid.

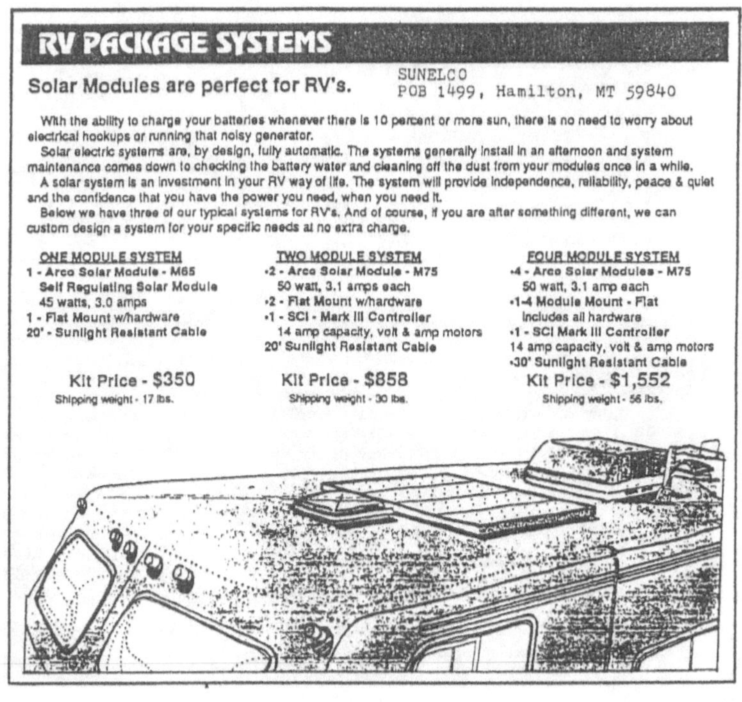

You can throw an old mattress and a sleeping bag into a VW van and call it "home" ... but actually trying to live in the stark little brute will be an uncomfortable experience. Or, if you have the bread, you can go to the other extreme and—for a few (or many) hundreds of dollars—buy and install a factory-built camper unit in your bug. The prefabbed interior—designed as it is for "average" needs—will probably never completely satisfy you, however ... and you'll find it dang difficult to remove when you want to use the VW for a little light hauling work.

My solution? A homemade conversion that includes:

- A bench seat that holds two comfortably

- A second bench seat for one

- A foldaway bed that sleeps two six-footers

- A fold-down work space in the back for cooking

- A magazine/book/map rack that keeps our current reading matter from getting trampled

- A large, hidden storage area for backpacks, fishing poles, etc., under the bed

- More covered storage space for clothes, shoes, books, gas cans, tools, etc., than the factory units offer.

If that isn't enough, this particular design seats seven people without removing anything (even our camping gear) and all we have to do to haul a sofa across town is spend less than one minute taking out the double bench seat (Unit F). For really massive moving jobs, we can remove the whole interior conversion in five to ten minutes without taking out a single nail or other fastener!

Was our wonder modification difficult and expensive to build? Not so's you'd notice. I put it together without plans in one month (including a full week for painting) and, until I started on the project, I'd never done any major carpentry work in my life. With the help of the drawings included here, you should beat my time by a wide margin. You might even bring in your conversion for less than the less-than-$25.00 we spent!

Just bear in mind that our VW van is a 1967 model and the dimensions shown on the accompanying illustrations

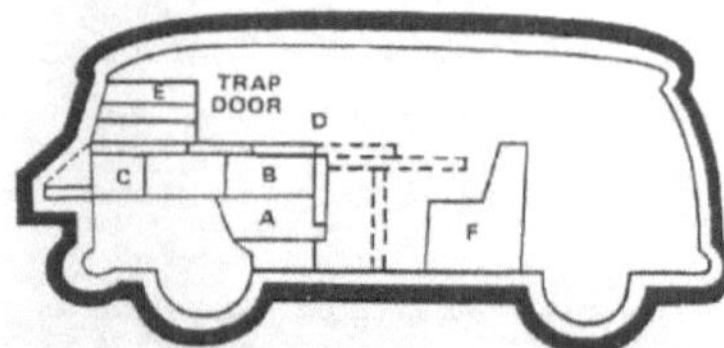

are only good for any bus or Kombi built before 1968. You'll have to cut into the wall padding in a few spots to make these units fit into a pre-1968 VW station wagon and Unit F will have to be altered for vans with bucket front seats if you want to preserve the walk space between them. Volkswagen buses built in 1968 or later have different internal dimensions than their older brothers so if you want to use this basic interior in them—and you can—you'll have to modify the measurements shown here accordingly.

Before you rush off to duplicate our success, however, I should tell you about the one drawback we've found with the design: We can't sit all the way up in bed. When you consider the mammoth storage space underneath the bunk, though, that's a relatively small price to pay.

LEFT: CROSS SECTION—SHOWING HOW ALL THE UNITS FIT TOGETHER TO GIVE YOU LOTS OF STORAGE SPACE.

OPPOSITE PAGE LEFT: BEDROOM—FOLD THE MATTRESS BACK AND YOU HAVE A DESK/DINING TABLE.

OPPOSITE PAGE RIGHT: LIVING ROOM—BED IS FOLDED DOWN TO COVER SHELVES AND GIVE MORE FLOOR SPACE.

BELOW: BASEMENT—TRAPDOOR COMPARTMENT UNDER THE BED FOR BACKPACKS, ETC.

BELOW RIGHT: KITCHEN—LOTS OF SHELVES PLUS A FOLD-OUT WORK SPACE.

MATERIALS:

- Two 4 X 8 sheets of 3/4-inch plywood (A-D exterior-type is best)
- An assortment of 3/4-inch plywood scraps (or another sheet of 4 X 8)
- Two strips of 1/4-inch plywood (at least 1 X 5)
- One bottle of Weldwood glue
- One box of no. 4 finishing nails
- A dozen 5/8-inch wood screws
- Two 1/4-inch by 4-inch bolts or pins
- Four small eye screws
- One yard of heavy twine (or three feet of light chain)
- One gallon of paint
- One pint of varnish
- Indoor-outdoor carpet scraps for a final touch of luxury

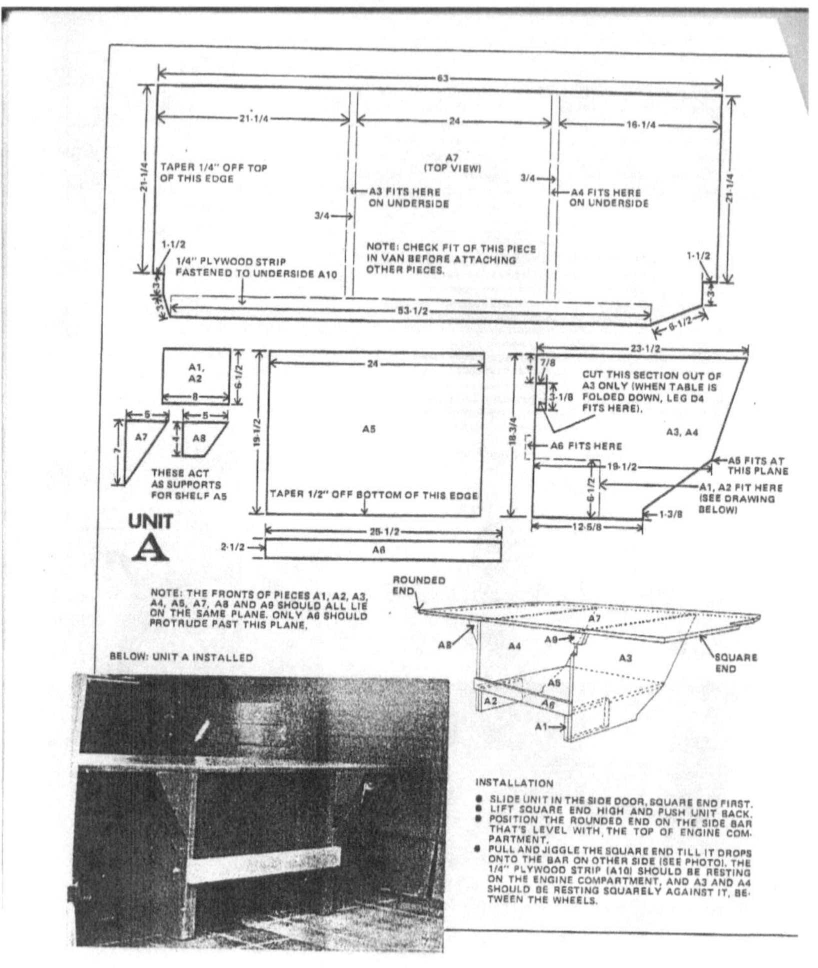

63
21-1/4
24
16-1/4
21-1/4
A7
(TOP VIEW)
TAPER 1/4" OFF TOP
OF THIS EDGE
3/4
A3 FITS HERE
ON UNDERSIDE
A4 FITS HERE
ON UNDERSIDE
21-1/4
3/4
1-1/2
1/4" PLYWOOD STRIP
FASTENED TO UNDERSIDE A10
NOTE: CHECK FIT OF THIS PIECE
IN VAN BEFORE ATTACHING
OTHER PIECES.
1-1/2
53-1/2
6-1/2
A1,
A2
6-1/2
8
24
23-1/2
7/8
CUT THIS SECTION OUT OF
A3 ONLY (WHEN TABLE IS
FOLDED DOWN, LEG D4
FITS HERE).
3-1/8
5
5
A7
4
A8
7
19-1/2
A5
18-3/4
A3, A4
A6 FITS HERE
A5 FITS AT
THIS PLANE
THESE ACT
AS SUPPORTS
FOR SHELF A5
TAPER 1/2" OFF BOTTOM OF THIS EDGE
19-1/2
6-1/2
A1, A2 FIT HERE
(SEE DRAWING
BELOW)
UNIT
A
25-1/2
12-5/8
1-3/8
2-1/2
A6
NOTE: THE FRONTS OF PIECES A1, A2, A3,
A4, A5, A7, A8 AND A9 SHOULD ALL LIE
ON THE SAME PLANE. ONLY A6 SHOULD
PROTRUDE PAST THIS PLANE.
BELOW: UNIT A INSTALLED
ROUNDED
END
A7
A8
A4
A9
A3
SQUARE
END
A5
A2
A6
A1
INSTALLATION
SLIDE UNIT IN THE SIDE DOOR, SQUARE END FIRST.
LIFT SQUARE END HIGH AND PUSH UNIT BACK.
POSITION THE ROUNDED END ON THE SIDE BAR
THAT'S LEVEL WITH THE TOP OF ENGINE COM-
PARTMENT.
PULL AND JIGGLE THE SQUARE END TILL IT DROPS
ONTO THE BAR ON OTHER SIDE (SEE PHOTO). THE
1/4" PLYWOOD STRIP (A10) SHOULD BE RESTING
ON THE ENGINE COMPARTMENT, AND A3 AND A4
SHOULD BE RESTING SQUARELY AGAINST IT, BE-
TWEEN THE WHEELS.

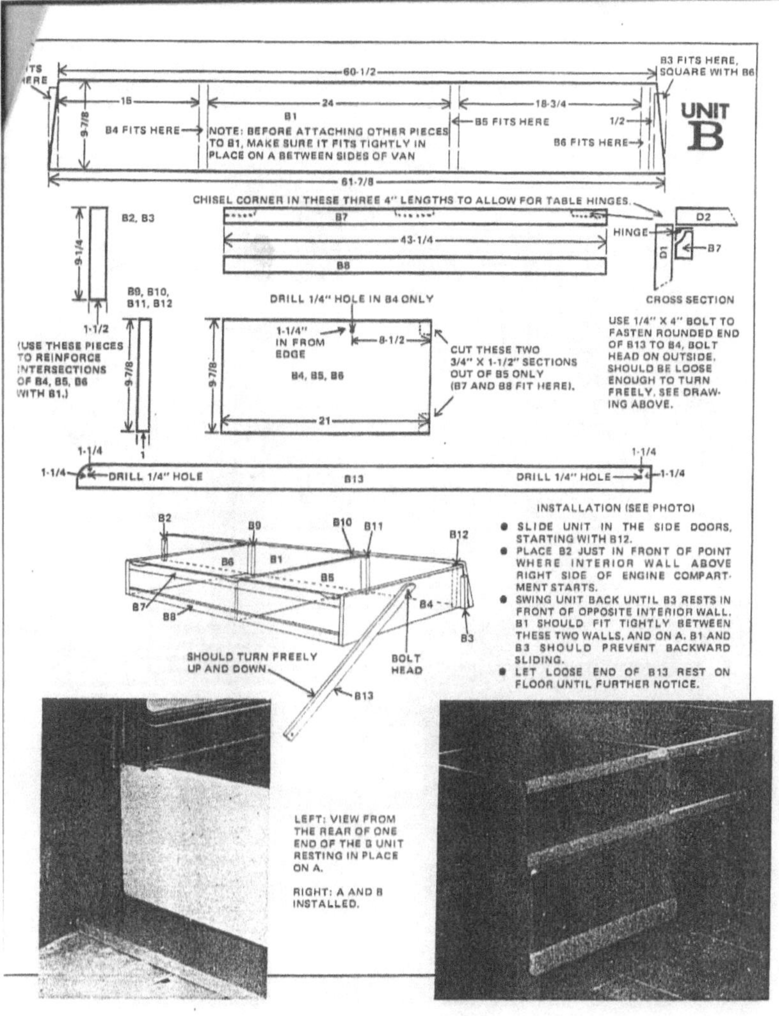
B3 FITS HERE, SQUARE WITH B6
FITS HERE
60-1/2
18
24
18-3/4
1/2
UNIT B
B1
9-7/8
B4 FITS HERE
NOTE: BEFORE ATTACHING OTHER PIECES TO B1, MAKE SURE IT FITS TIGHTLY IN PLACE ON A BETWEEN SIDES OF VAN
B5 FITS HERE
B6 FITS HERE
61-7/8
CHISEL CORNER IN THESE THREE 4" LENGTHS TO ALLOW FOR TABLE HINGES.
B2, B3
9-1/4
B9, B10, B11, B12
1-1/2
(USE THESE PIECES TO REINFORCE INTERSECTIONS OF B4, B5, B6 WITH B1.)
9-7/8
1-1/4
1
B7
43-1/4
B8
D2
HINGE
D1
B7
CROSS SECTION
DRILL 1/4" HOLE IN B4 ONLY
1-1/4" IN FROM EDGE
8-1/2
9-7/8
B4, B5, B6
CUT THESE TWO 3/4" X 1-1/2" SECTIONS OUT OF B5 ONLY (B7 AND B8 FIT HERE).
21
USE 1/4" X 4" BOLT TO FASTEN ROUNDED END OF B13 TO B4, BOLT HEAD ON OUTSIDE. SHOULD BE LOOSE ENOUGH TO TURN FREELY. SEE DRAWING ABOVE.
1-1/4
1-1/4
1-1/4
DRILL 1/4" HOLE
B13
DRILL 1/4" HOLE
1-1/4
B2
B9
B10
B11
B12
B6
B1
B5
B7
B8
B4
B3
SHOULD TURN FREELY UP AND DOWN
BOLT HEAD
B13
INSTALLATION (SEE PHOTO)
SLIDE UNIT IN THE SIDE DOORS, STARTING WITH B12.
PLACE B2 JUST IN FRONT OF POINT WHERE INTERIOR WALL ABOVE RIGHT SIDE OF ENGINE COMPARTMENT STARTS.
SWING UNIT BACK UNTIL B3 RESTS IN FRONT OF OPPOSITE INTERIOR WALL. B1 SHOULD FIT TIGHTLY BETWEEN THESE TWO WALLS, AND ON A. B1 AND B3 SHOULD PREVENT BACKWARD SLIDING.
LET LOOSE END OF B13 REST ON FLOOR UNTIL FURTHER NOTICE.
LEFT: VIEW FROM THE REAR OF ONE END OF THE B UNIT RESTING IN PLACE ON A.
RIGHT: A AND B INSTALLED.

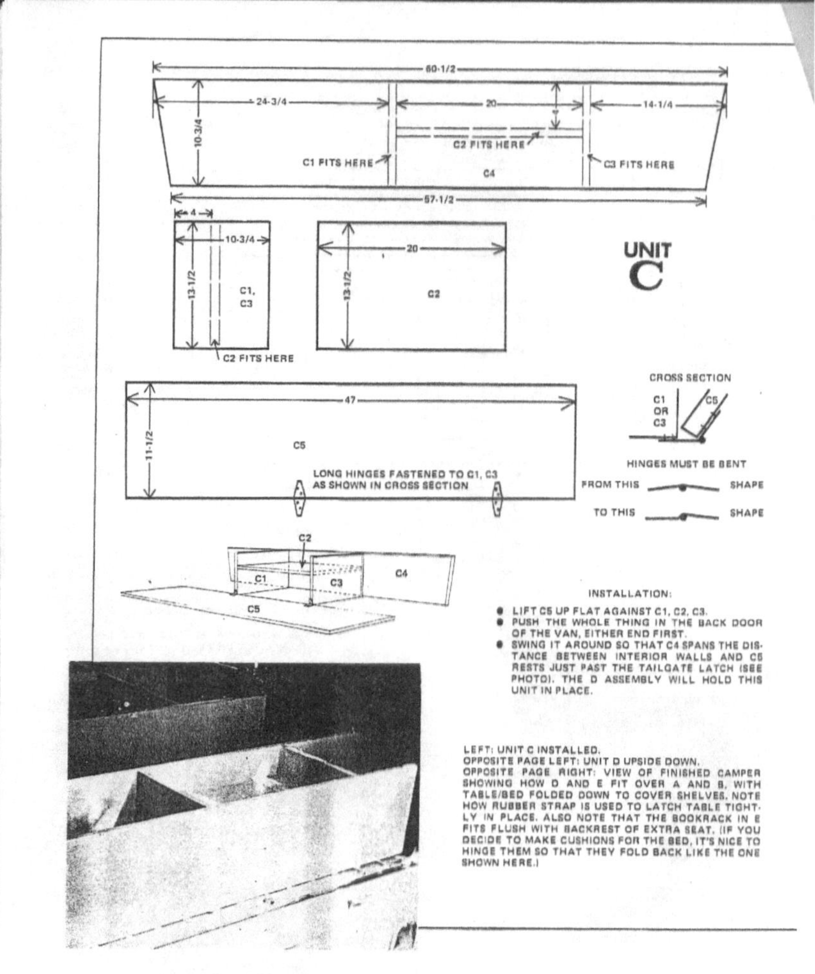

INSTALLATION:

- LIFT C5 UP FLAT AGAINST C1, C2, C3.
- PUSH THE WHOLE THING IN THE BACK DOOR OF THE VAN, EITHER END FIRST.
- SWING IT AROUND SO THAT C4 SPANS THE DISTANCE BETWEEN INTERIOR WALLS AND C5 RESTS JUST PAST THE TAILGATE LATCH (SEE PHOTO). THE D ASSEMBLY WILL HOLD THIS UNIT IN PLACE.

LEFT: UNIT C INSTALLED.
OPPOSITE PAGE LEFT: UNIT D UPSIDE DOWN.
OPPOSITE PAGE RIGHT: VIEW OF FINISHED CAMPER SHOWING HOW D AND E FIT OVER A AND B, WITH TABLE/BED FOLDED DOWN TO COVER SHELVES. NOTE HOW RUBBER STRAP IS USED TO LATCH TABLE TIGHTLY IN PLACE. ALSO NOTE THAT THE BOOKRACK IN E FITS FLUSH WITH BACKREST OF EXTRA SEAT. (IF YOU DECIDE TO MAKE CUSHIONS FOR THE BED, IT'S NICE TO HINGE THEM SO THAT THEY FOLD BACK LIKE THE ONE SHOWN HERE.)

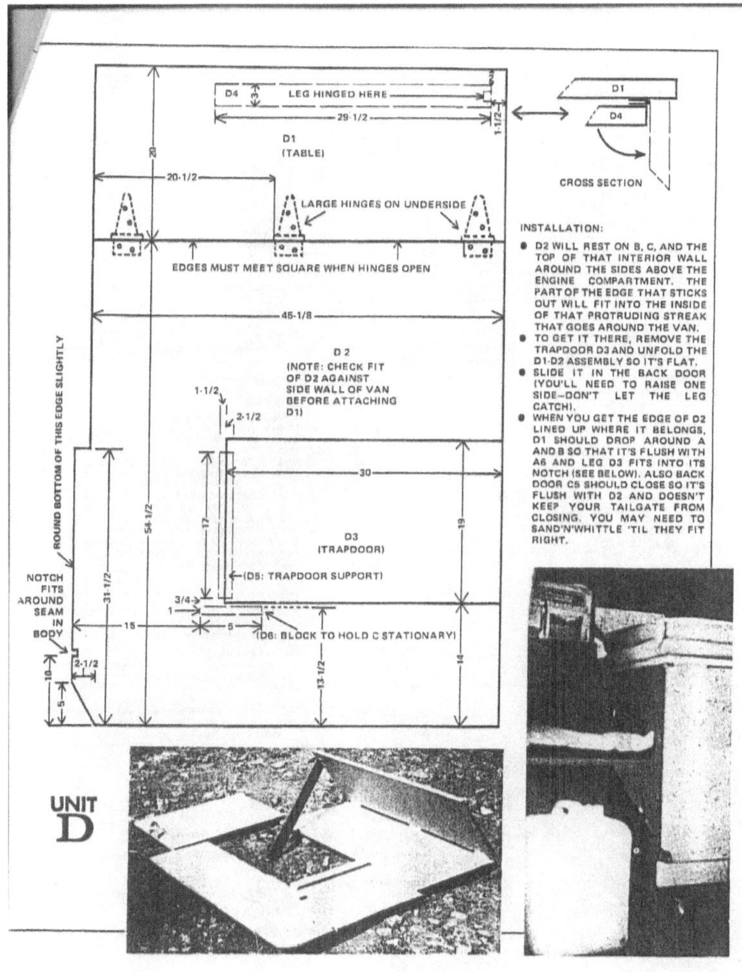

INSTALLATION:

- D2 WILL REST ON B, C, AND THE TOP OF THAT INTERIOR WALL AROUND THE SIDES ABOVE THE ENGINE COMPARTMENT. THE PART OF THE EDGE THAT STICKS OUT WILL FIT INTO THE INSIDE OF THAT PROTRUDING STREAK THAT GOES AROUND THE VAN.
- TO GET IT THERE, REMOVE THE TRAPDOOR D3 AND UNFOLD THE D1-D2 ASSEMBLY SO IT'S FLAT.
- SLIDE IT IN THE BACK DOOR (YOU'LL NEED TO RAISE ONE SIDE—DON'T LET THE LEG CATCH).
- WHEN YOU GET THE EDGE OF D2 LINED UP WHERE IT BELONGS, D1 SHOULD DROP AROUND A AND B SO THAT IT'S FLUSH WITH A6 AND LEG D3 FITS INTO ITS NOTCH (SEE BELOW). ALSO BACK DOOR C5 SHOULD CLOSE SO IT'S FLUSH WITH D2 AND DOESN'T KEEP YOUR TAILGATE FROM CLOSING. YOU MAY NEED TO SAND'N'WHITTLE 'TIL THEY FIT RIGHT.

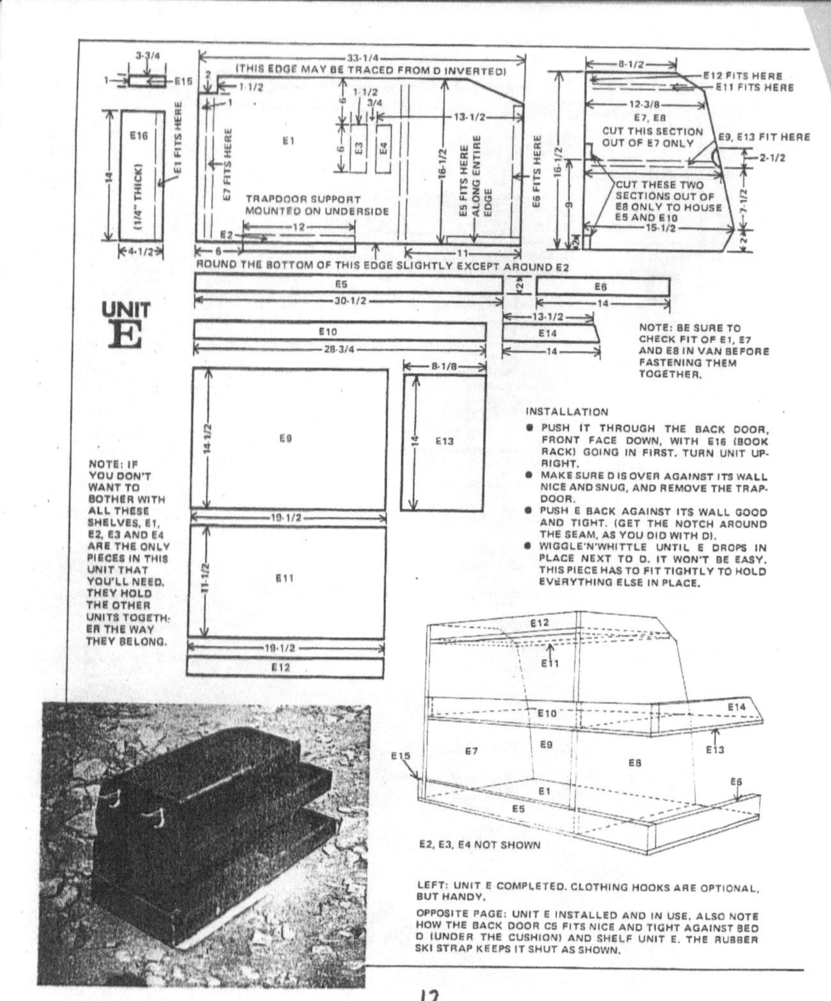

LEFT: UNIT E COMPLETED. CLOTHING HOOKS ARE OPTIONAL, BUT HANDY.

OPPOSITE PAGE: UNIT E INSTALLED AND IN USE. ALSO NOTE HOW THE BACK DOOR C5 FITS NICE AND TIGHT AGAINST BED D (UNDER THE CUSHION) AND SHELF UNIT E. THE RUBBER SKI STRAP KEEPS IT SHUT AS SHOWN.

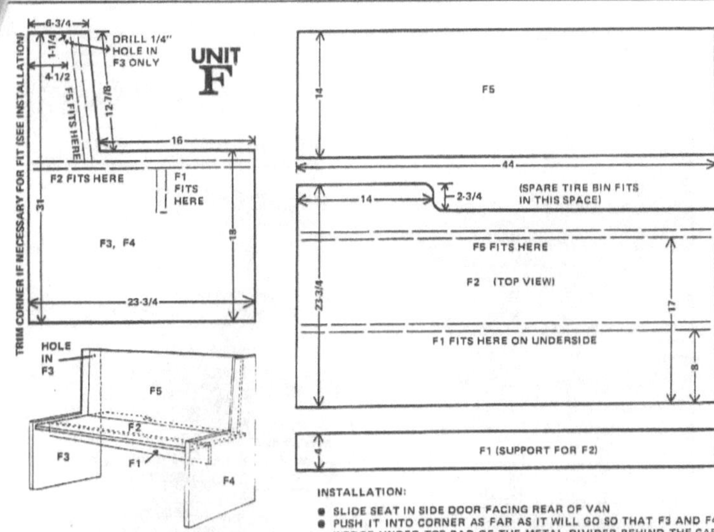

INSTALLATION:

- SLIDE SEAT IN SIDE DOOR FACING REAR OF VAN
- PUSH IT INTO CORNER AS FAR AS IT WILL GO SO THAT F3 AND F4 WEDGE UNDER TOP BAR OF THE METAL DIVIDER BEHIND THE CAB (SEE PHOTO OF LIVING ROOM, PAGE 87).

FINISHING TOUCHES

NOW YOU'VE JUST GOT THE DETAILS TO TAKE CARE OF:

- PUT THE EYE SCREWS AND CHAINS ON BOTH SIDES OF THE REAR KITCHEN DOOR AND FASTEN THE OTHER ENDS WITH EYE SCREWS TO THE D AND E UNITS, AS SHOWN IN THE KITCHEN PHOTO (PAGE 86). MAKE THE CHAINS JUST LONG ENOUGH TO LET THE DOOR DROP TO A FLAT WORK SPACE.
- PUT A HANDLE ON THE TRAPDOOR (ROPE, FABRIC, ETC.).
- USE THE SCREWS AND RUBBER SKI FASTENERS AS LATCHES TO HOLD THE KITCHEN DOOR CLOSED AND THE TABLE DOWN. I'LL LET YOU AND THE PHOTOS WORK THIS ONE OUT TOGETHER.
- CHECK OUT THE SUPPORTS FOR THE BED/TABLE. FIRST LIFT THE TABLE UP FLAT AND LET THE LEG HOLD IT UP. NOW SWING THAT LONG ARM (B13—REMEMBER?) UP 'TIL IT'S LEVEL. THE OTHER 4" BOLT SHOULD FIT THROUGH THE HOLE IN THE SIDE OF THE BENCH AND THE HOLE IN THE END OF THE ARM TO SUPPORT THE TABLE. IF THE TWO HOLES DON'T MEET SQUARELY YOU'LL HAVE TO MOVE ONE OF THEM.
- DON'T FORGET THE PAINT!
- WE MADE SNAP-TOGETHER FOAM-RUBBER CUSHIONS TO FIT THE BED SEGMENTS. WE ALSO INSTALLED AN OLD MEDICINE CHEST NEXT TO THE BENCH. WE FOUND SOME OLD WOODEN MILK AND PEPSI CRATES THAT FIT NICELY UNDER THE BENCH AND MAKE GREAT CLOTHES BINS. BUT YOU'RE THE ONE WHO'LL BE LIVING IN YOURS, SO I'LL LET YOU FIGURE OUT WHAT EXTRAS BEST FIT YOUR TRAVELING NEEDS. HAPPY TRAILS!

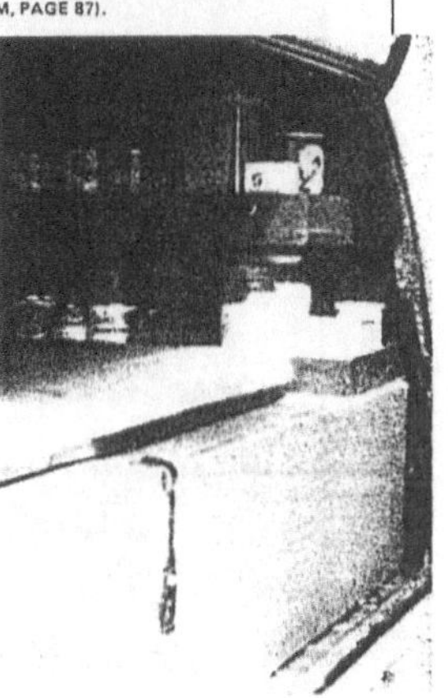

13

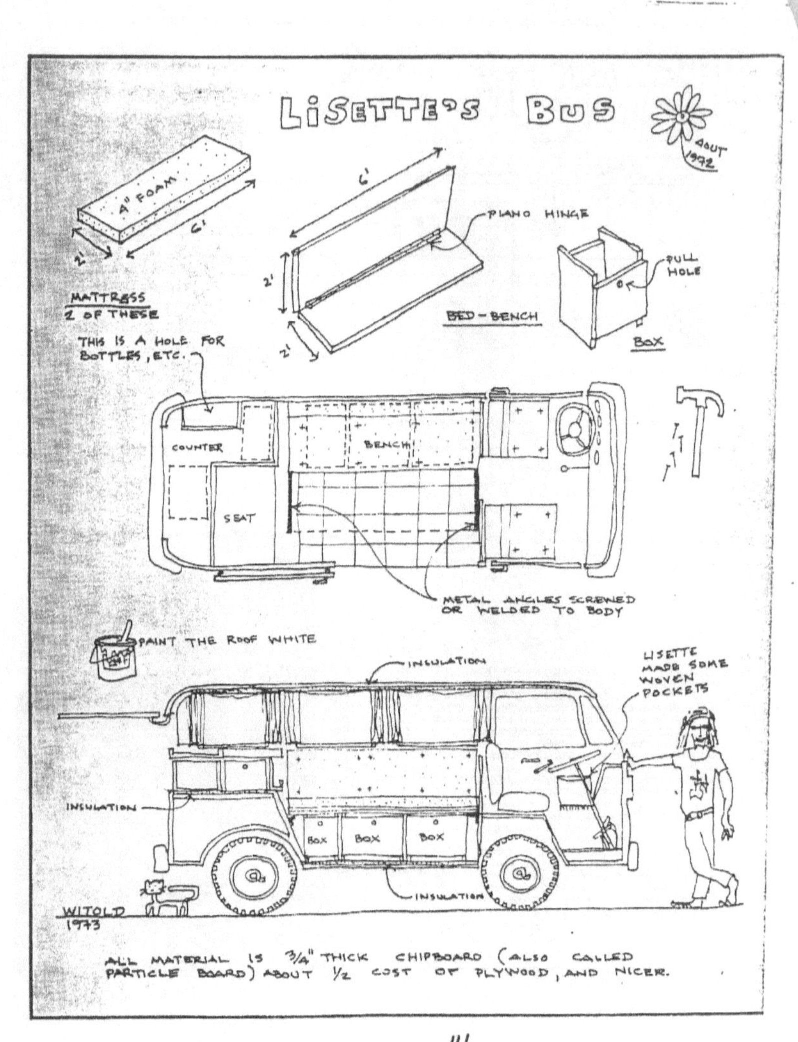

LISETTE'S BUS
AOUT 1992
4" FOAM
6'
2'
MATTRESS
2 OF THESE
PIANO HINGE
2'
2'
BED - BENCH
PULL HOLE
BOX
THIS IS A HOLE FOR BOTTLES, ETC.
COUNTER
BENCH
SEAT
METAL ANGLES SCREWED OR WELDED TO BODY
PAINT THE ROOF WHITE
INSULATION
LISETTE MADE SOME WOVEN POCKETS
INSULATION
BOX   BOX   BOX
INSULATION
WITOLD 1973
ALL MATERIAL IS 3/4" THICK CHIPBOARD (ALSO CALLED PARTICLE BOARD) ABOUT 1/2 COST OF PLYWOOD, AND NICER.

FEEDBACK ON THE VW BUS CONVERSION

George Berkman's article on his design for a VW Campmobile with removable components (LIFESTYLE! NO. 4) made me wonder whether LIFESTYLE!'s readers would be interested in other ways of converting buses.

Last summer I built a modification for the VW that took my friend Lisette from Montreal to Louisiana to Boulder and eventually back. The advantage of my design is that you don't sleep with your nose against the ceiling...instead, the bed is 20 inches off the floor and doubles as a bench. The mattress is two portions so your seat has a padded back as well.

The bunk slides freely on two pieces of angle iron that are screwed or welded to the car body, one to the rear of the seats and the other to the sloped part over the engine. When the hinged panels are slid forward they become a bed...and they're easily removed. It's very important to have storage boxes under the bunk to help support it.

The various containers and drawers I've indicated should be sized to store whatever you have: dishes, clothes, stove, food, etc.

In my conversion all parts are made of chipboard, which is easy to cut, glue and nail...and which is attractive when varnished. It's also much cheaper than plywood and ecologically sounder, being made of waste chips and glue.

One very important point which George didn't mention in his article is the insulation that is necessary to make the bus livable in a hot or cold climate. One-inch styrofoam on the ceiling, floor and walls will help keep the inside temperature comfortable and will also dampen the sound of the engine. Painting the van's roof white makes for a cooler interior.

One hint: The bus is full of odd bumps and curves. Cutting shapes out of cardboard first and fitting the pieces will save you a lot of time.

Witold Rybczynski
Minimum Cost Housing Group
School of Architecture
McGill University
Montreal, Canada

JOEL RANDALL (PREFORM-INFORM)

July 11, 1969 was my last day of institutionalized employment. After selling most of our personal items and organizing the balance, we moved on.

Our living quarters are a 1966 Avion 25-foot single axle travel trailer. We purchased the unit used and added on folding bunk beds and dinette seats to the folding leaf table and two single bed already in the trailer. With this arrangement we are able to sleep six. The space is small for two adults and four children ranging in age from 4 to 10 but we have pretty well adjusted except for my wife's occasional bouts of cabin fever.

We are self-contained with water storage, holding tank, 12-volt lighting system complete with a storage battery backed with a 110-volt charger, gas or electric refrigerator, gas heat, gas water heater, gas stove and oven, three exhaust fans (all 12 volt) and a 110 volt refrigeration unit. Refrigeration is a near necessity, rather than a luxury, for six people living in close quarters.

Our tow rig is a 1965 International Travelall which is almost ideal for pulling the trailer as its drive train and suspension is built on the order of a light truck. We have adequate room for passengers with an extra two seats, storage and an elevated foam pad supported by plywood and legs above the storage area in the rear. The two-inch pad makes a nice bed for either children or an adult while we're traveling.

Our Travelall has a 266 cubic inch V8 engine and a 3-speed standard transmission. I would recommend a larger V8 of over 300 cubic inches and a 4-speed transmission to others planning our heavy use of a vehicle. Four wheel drive is a necessity for any off-road trailering. The Travelall is a comfortable, useable auto when unhooked from the trailer and, in my opinion, it's a mistake to plan a lot of trailering with a standard automobile. A car purchased as a factory tow vehicle might be alright but a standard auto will have problems such as overheating, drive train failures (especially in the transmission), weak suspension, and brake and wheel overloading.

We've towed over 5,000 miles in our trailer for over 2 months now. Our travel speed is generally 50 to 55 mph if road and traffic conditions allow. We can pull much faster but the gas consumption increases greatly and the higher speeds are much harder on all the equipment. Increased speed also increases possibilities for accidents. Since we have no deadlines, there isn't any hurry for us.

Our only negative experience while traveling was the result of human error in Utah. We took a shortcut that resulted in our backing down a two-mile-long curved mountain grade that we were unable to pull. It was much too far down over the edge for comfort, I might add. We later made the grade by dumping water and the holding tank and taking a run in low with the engine overspeeded (4500 rpm).

We have stayed in roadside rest areas, KOA-type campgrounds, gas stations, socialist parks, private public parks provided by service clubs, city streets, Indian reservations, road ditches and many places of unknown ownership. We try to keep costs at a minimum and usually park at no cost. We've found ample parking spots in the Midwest where many towns and service clubs provide no-charge areas. For example, we've stayed overnight at the Sydney, Nebraska fairgrounds were we even had electricity and water at no charge. No one patrolled the area and there were no posted limitations on the time one could stay.

Our luxury equipment consists of a portable tape stereo and a portable TV. The stereo is a Concord Model F400 made by Panasonic of Japan. It operates on 110 or 6 "D" cells. We have recorded 50 hours of cassette tape from our records. Our TV operates on 12 volt or 110 and we can use it in either the trailer or the Travelall. We are not inclined to watch large amounts of TV but it does provide diversion while traveling.

During the summer our income will be from labor here in Nebraska. My father has a farm and ranch where I'm able to work the whole family part time and myself as much as desired. Our cost of living is low and we'll coast during the winter, earning a few bucks where and whenever possible.

Shortly after the first of October we plan to travel to the east coast, follow the coast line south to Florida and west along the Gulf to Mississippi. We will go as far and as quickly as we desire, depending on our whims at the time. We plan to license our rig in Mississippi or Virginia as neither state has compulsory socialist education.

Someday, when finances and experience allow, we hope to acquire a trimaran and do our wandering on the oceans, cruising the West Indies and possibly sailing to the South Sea Islands.

We've been very busy getting equipped and organized the past few months but the whole thing has been very enjoyable to me. I feel that I'm just beginning to live.

PETER (PREFORM-INFORM)

My wife, two-year-old child and I presently live in a 22-foot, chassis mounted, channeled-through motor home on a one-ton Ford truck. We've been in this rig for the last eight months. Before that we lived in a 21-foot trailer for a year.

I am able to earn an above-average living in the Chicago area in the summer by plying my trade of paperhanging. I have been able to do as well in the winter in Miami, Florida. Being able to make contacts in this field as an independent contractor, I could — if others were interested — provide a means of making money for a caravan. I know the market in this trade and feel that if three to five men were to form a contracting-decorating service to work in the larger urban areas it would take — at most — two months to fill the next egg for the families involved. I am not well versed in forage living but, if I were more knowledgeable in that field, I am sure that less "outside" income would be needed.

We have traveled to the middle west, southwest, south and east coast and — to our amazement — we've only been told to move on twice on two years. This is most surprising for we are quite longhaired and I have a beard. I am sure, due to the ever-growing alertness of our nation's paranoids, that this sort of luck can't last long.

We are neither far left nor right. We won't be part of anything where guns do the talking, and today they talk from both sides. The thing for us to do, I guess, is stay out of the way — if that's possible — and let the guns take care of each other.

TOM TERRIFIC (INNOVATOR)

The primary gratis rental for the nomad and/or remote traveler is absentee-owned land. Roads and fences to be repaired, cattle watched and timber guarded are only a few reasons that absentee land owners seek farm and ranch caretakers.

How does one find such a deal? First, try the local newspapers (not only the dailies but the weeklies and "throw aways" too) of the area in which you want to locate. Bulletin board notices (the best place for these – according to a land owner – are saddle shops and auction yards) can also be productive. When you run an ad or post a notice, state what you're looking for and what you are willing to do. There's no need to post a philosophical treatise: The folks you want to reach have little time for such subjects. The next step – and usually the most successful – is going out and looking and asking.

In small towns, ask the police or storekeepers or local ranchers. Few people will get uptight if you let it be known that you're willing to work in exchange for living space. Country shopkeepers are often local real estate dealers; check them. Realtors use caretakers too. Visit farms and ranches to pick up the gossip and needs of the neighborhood.

Gratis rent isn't a fantasy to dream about. It's happened to friends: One group I know was invited to live on a ranch by a land owner who digs "drop outs." An acquaintance got a house in the woods for repairs and improvements on the building. Another caretakes a house and land in exchange for rent.

Me? I turned down an offer to park my camper gratis in the mountains while cutting wood for a living. Instead I moved the rig, my family and myself to another mountain top where I live – without rent – in 77 acres of forest. I neither have to work...nor not work...traveling slowly...being free.

BILL LULAY (PREFORM-INFORM)

We have been living in our school bus-converted-to-camper for six months now and doing very well. After I left Xerox, I took a job for three weeks with the Woodstock Music and Arts Festival in Bethal, N.Y. We are actually trying to find a commune to live in but, even if we do, we'll probably remain fairly mobile.

We have lately been turned on to the number of wild plants that grow all over the country and which are there for the picking. Frequently, well over half a meal can be prepared from them. Meat is getting so expensive as to make it fairly scarce on our table. Oatmeal is a good, cheap, basic food which can be fixed with a variety of additives (honey, sugar, maple sugar, raisins, molasses, fruit, leftovers...you name it.)

Since leaving Xerox we've gotten really good at living cheaply. We just bought an armful of heavy used clothing and used the material to make winter clothes for our 2-1/2-year-old daughter. Cost: a couple of bucks plus the time spent sewing.

Our school bus gets about 6 or 7 miles to the gallon and we both have bikes (bicycles, not motor bikes which cost money in repairs, service and fuel) on which we travel away from the bus.

On a recent trip to Canada we stopped overnight at highway rest areas. Although this is illegal (and one of them had a notice saying so) we were never hassled by the cops. If we weren't in a hurry, we'd stay until afternoon from the previous night's stop, then do just an hour or less driving before pulling into another spot to eat supper and spend the night. Prices of everything varied considerably from the southern to the northern part of New York State. Food generally got cheaper as we went north and gas became more expensive. Oh well...just some handy dandy tips, folks, for living with as little expenditure as possible.

We found it necessary, on trying to enter Canada, to fabricate a job and story about being on vacation in order to satisfy the up-tight 40-hour-per-week immigration shlub who feared we were trying to sneak into the country to live permanently. Apparently it looked to him like we had all our worldly possessions with us (which, of course, we did). I now have a friend who will verify that I am working for him and that we live in an apartment in the back of his shop. Many straight people, especially those in authority, get very upset if it appears that you not only don't have a job and no permanent residence...but that you enjoy it immensely and don't WANT a job or permanent residence.

The main barriers to this form of self-liberation are psychologic. People who think nothing of living for two weeks in a camping vehicle will come up with fifty million objections for extending that two weeks to forever. They'll tell you it's IMPOSSIBLE to live in a vehicle. I suspect the insecurity of having no place (piece of ground) to call home upsets them. This lack of security can't be dismissed too lightly.

TWO LETTERS FROM AL FRY

During the last ten years I have spent less than a dozen dollars a week on average for direct living expense. My son and I have survived nicely over this period and enjoyed ourselves to boot. After a beatnik period and much discomfort we found that the ideal ace in the hole is a bread delivery van. Anyone who *really* applies himself can get the shekels together to buy one and most leasing companies in any large city will have used trucks (which they've leased to bakeries) for sale. Bread vans are going toward diesel engines because it cuts costs almost in half. Such a used vehicle at any reasonable price is really a hidden gem.

I passed through various stages of step-in vans but finally settled upon a truck with the whole works, paneling and all. Although I have had a lot of portable stoves and closets which served well (some motor vehicle departments don't check out your modifications so it's up to you to decide how far you want to go). The Big Three improvements are (1) toilet, (2) water and (3) fuel (gas or ?) in that order.

At this writing a Porta Potti is the best self-contained privy on the market (at a steep $100) but any air-tight can may be used as a chemical toilet if it is laced with Chlorox once a day. With this solved, water is no problem: A cheap plastic Jerry can and hand pump will do the job. A small propane stove will handle the last detail and it's surprising how well a wood stove works: Some coal or hard wood banked up keeps you warm all night, and everywhere you go there is wood for the gathering. Put a screen over the top of the stovepipe to arrest sparks, watch where you park and you'll sniff the woodsy smell just enough to learn to love it.

I have a little French Citroen which I pull behind me wherever I go. Cycles are easier but I like my comfort and, at 50 miles per gallon, I can afford the nuisance of towing my little friend along.

California is "my state" and I often feel like a stay in Los Angeles or San Francisco where I am near either water or some of the action that is always going on. Los Angeles has a few places under freeways in the Hollywood area that are good for a week or so until you make contact with a safer area. Sausalito, near San Francisco, is a mecca for bohemian wanderers and you will often see the ultimate in "way out" mobile homes thereabouts although property owners are getting a little hardnosed in recent years.

My usual procedure for extended stay is to put a mental order in for what I want and then try to spot a fenced-in "safe area" that looks like it needs guarding, protection...or squatting on. With a little inquiry it usually isn't long before you have a safe place to park...often complete with electricity and hose water. A couple of hours a week of helping, handyman work or whatever usually suffices for rent. I have camped with permission "gypsy style" near some of California's most interesting areas. I've found quite a few "safe camping zones" in southern California and many thousands available with a little digging and permission hunting.

The desert is full of beautiful places and surprises. An old favorite of mine when coming or going is Whitewater River Canyon about 10 miles north of Palm Springs just off Indio Freeway. The river runs the year around there and the only hang up is occasional wind.

Did you ever get hung up staying around a hot spring? Let me say that is my idea of good times: freedom and warm relaxation. There's a spring in the hills about six miles back of Santa Barbara where the local bohemian element takes midnight skinny dips. Another is fitted as a public camp two miles off the road about 20 miles this side of Lone Pine. In northern California, Idaho and other areas of the Pacific Northwest there are oodles of hot springs. Many are not dammed or tanked but I have camped many enjoyable days around improvised tub resting in a primeval little meadow...

After finding my domicile it took me years to learn that you can't stay healthy on human food from stores: Every additive is a poison as far as I'm concerned now. If one gets some green foliage of some kind into his system every day and stops eating sugar, he will beat viruses and most other bugs. Most edible weeds taste great mixed with a little pineapple juice and blended in the blender. You can get good brown rice, lima beans and other healthful staples for around $10 a hundred from the right milling outfit in any large city. You can exist exclusively on alkaline grains and beans and thrive whereas you'll get sick fast eating only wheat flour and its products. My waffle iron makes me delicious waffles out of any kind of thing I want to grind up in my little health-foodstore grinder. Bone meal from a feed store mixed with custard and dried in the sun (to make it palatable) will end forever any trips to your dentist, providing you don't allow tooth calcium leaching due to a very high acid food (wheat, sugar, meat) diet.

Many women have enjoyed sharing my rambling life and girls all over the country are now going the "gypsy way" but, generally speaking, the propaganda of the Big American Dream has taken a heavier toll among women than among men. The times are achangin', however. I have met retired couples (even under retirement age) who travel from town to town, working a while at the lower paying jobs and moving on again...convinced they should have done it years ago. Kids love this way of life and my son is probably as well-rounded as a son of one of the Jet Set.

Our thrift shop clothes – thanks to a little sewing machine work – are the latest thing. With no rent, little food costs and a trifling gas bill I haven't been gainfully employed for a stereotype boss in years. By choice, the dollars seem to come in through helping people who ask...or through odd coincidental bumbling. It's really only a case of application and accepting a lot less than the next guy gets (and must spend pronto).

Remember, no other nation in the world has thousands of used transportation cars for so little or refrigerators, ranges and appliances available used and secondhand so cheap. It's incredible. You can enjoy life no matter what the brain washers say...And everything enjoyed is greater when shared. My greatest moments were usually spent in modest surroundings with good company...good conversation...guitar picking...philosophical feasts.

Some people are born with itchy feet and are generally discontented. For such people, being tied to the normal routine is a prison. What amazes me is that so many of these folks resign themselves to it. After knocking around this country and a few of the World's "last frontier/paradise" spots for some years I am convinced that almost anyone – regardless of education or burdens – can live a satisfying, reasonably comfortable life the "Gypsy Way".

I've tried a number of approaches but, in a nutshell, I think the most comfortable way to live on the road is by investing in a mobile, self-propelled home from a converted bus or van. At this moment I could pick up a number of such vehicles within a 20-mile radius for less than a thousand dollars apiece. If you hoard a little away and wait for the right deal, you'll find there are some fantastic bargains available.

I personally favor the converted step-vans but, if I had more than my one son, I suspect I would try to get a small Greyhound-type bus which has so much more room at the expense of conspicuousness and gas economy. I have met a number of New Gypsys with these big rigs and some have put in a workshop in which they do leather, jewelry, paintings and whatnot to help pay for their gas along the road. Some hit the national parks and tourist spots. Others work with the more bohemian centers or just sell their wares the itinerant way.

Once you've made the initial investment, whether for a banged up van (with a decent engine) at a couple of hundred dollars or for a ten thousand dollar commercially-manufactured motor home, the rest is easy. Adjustment is mainly mental and this can be helped by absorbing the information in MOTHER [Earth News] or any of the other back-to-the-land material now around for the looking. If money is scarce, sit tight until you can get a little nest egg ahead for emergencies. While you're waiting you can outfit your home on wheels.

Conversion is easy and you'll find lots of room under the floor of your particular rig. As an example, I have a small, stripped down water heater mounted to the frame of my van and it provides outdoor hot showers when I'm plugged in to service outlets. It also holds spare water when I'm on the road. I have a lot of tools and paint under my camper's floorboards too and they make me extra dollars when I spy a painting or sign job to be done.

Getting the hardware you need such as kerosene or propane lamps, stoves and heaters is usually simple and inexpensive at swap meets, flea markets and junk stores. This is the fun part and I have hardware that is as high camp as the imagination can conceive. If you have room for instance, a little wood-burning stove is really a fine thing to have in your van, novel as it may seem.

Your portable toilet can be a chemically laced (most cheap disinfectants will work) airtight G.I. ammo box, plastic pail...or the superb (and expensive) Porti-Potti available from trailer supply houses.

No matter what your rig is, it will be simply amazing the amount of stuff you'll be able to cram in, under and on it...providing the vehicle has the bearings to take it. I've found, as a general rule of thumb, that if our mobile cabin has tires rated eight ply or better mounted on wheels with eight lug bolts (a pretty standard truck setup), the machine will probably carry (and carry safely) any of the comforts of home you're likely to pack aboard. You may want to add coil springs to protect the frame if you really travel heavy, but, otherwise, weight should never be a problem.

There is one problem to prepare for in advance, however, and that is the fact that the "no overnight camping in our town" laws are occasionally enforced. Getting rousted out of a city in the middle of the night can be depressing and is probably entirely unnecessary if you have your water storage, portable toilet and blackout window problems worked out before you find yourself on a less-than-friendly city street.

The water and toilet aspects are already solved if you have designed overnight self-sufficiency into your vehicle and the windows can be taken care of with covers of heavy black plastic applied as tightly as possible to the panes. You'll also find it a good idea to skip a couple side windows and install a large skylight on top of your rig when you're converting it. Your camper's interior will be brighter during the day and you'll have fewer windows to seal at night.

If you have the bread to bypass a converted rig and you're in the market for a manufactured motor home, I advise buying a model with dual wheels for traction and lugging heavy loads, a small six engine for economy (a diesel is even better), at least four speeds forward for steep grades and a body roomy up to the point of ill balance.

There is nothing preventing a good life on the road except a lack of guts and gall. Things work out if you try and jobs are easy to find. Maybe you see a road being built in pretty country and you stop and apply for work...or you notice a sign that needs retouching or a building with peeling paint and you give the owner a price for fixing it. There are temporary jobs all over if your attire and smile fit the part.

We come and go as we please in our van and we prefer to live a while in the city and a while in the country. Finding an overnight spot in the city is usually no trouble but longer stays usually take a little scrounging, permission getting, friend making and such. The country is no problem. I prefer to ramble the west and have dozens of secluded and abandoned homesteads, ranches and squat spots where I can grow a garden and enjoy the summer before heading to warmer areas in the winter.

I know several ghost towns in Idaho that are fantastic for the summer. For example, the Boise Basin near Idaho City has a number of easily accessible abandoned towns as does a good portion of the northwest. These places will be gone someday except in a rich memory.

While I haven't traipsed around the eastern part of the country for a time, I remember some very inviting hideaways from Arkansas on east; places that only a smile and permission would have opened for a lengthy stay...or spots that were just there to be used for the night.

We used to work summers in the northwestern United States and go south – often Mexico – in the winter. Now it seems I am slowing down and getting involved in causes to help our planet. It's almost as bad as a regular job except that I'm concerned and I think it's worth it and I do it by choice.

I can only repeat that the Gypsy Way is a good life if you just go do it. There will be ups and downs but that's true of whatever you do...and it's an open road across a lot of fantastic country.

BUS REBUILDING
By: Al Fry

Mobile living started for me the day I passed a car lot which had a dilapidated $150 travel trailer which I couldn't pass up for the price. I pulled it post haste to a friend's secluded orange orchard and decided that this sure might be the way to solve the problem of rent. One thing led to another and we would up pulling that trailer all over sunny Southern California, often sagging from the overload of junk or jetsam.

Pretty soon I got tired of trying to find suitable free spots to leave it while exploring an area or working, so we went on to an ancient U.P.S. truck which should have solved the problem but didn't. What it did do was point out the many mechanical problems one could run into. Sparing the details I hope that what scant bit of experience we later piled up will help someone else going the same path.

Several step-vans later I finally figured I had my ultimate vehicle when fate interceded again and I had a mate with a son and dogs. Well, to shorten the story, I laid out about 1500 bills with trembling fingers and became the hesitant owner of a gigantic 35 foot "48" Crown bus. Vans are one thing but flat-front buses are something else again.

Over the next six months or so we gained a lot of savvy on just how cheap one of these things can go together and still be presentable. The first surprising bit of luck was learning that one can usually get seconds and left overs from the trailer and camper builders who seem to be scattered all of S. Calif. Paneling for instance never ran us over a dollar a sheet and the more expensive hardware like sliding valve toilet, small water heater, and stove were usually less than a fourth of the new cost. An initial trip to our local dump quickly supplied us with the 2 x 4's and insulation to get things underway. ($2 a load is average scavenging rate.) Most of the lesser hardware came from swap meets where many trailer factory workers brought a lot of miscellaneous, and persons often unloaded unique gear from the past. Prize possessions on the "unique" list were one brass lever-handle water pump to supplement the electric jobby and various pieces of antique hardware and bric-a-brac.

I have always searched high and low to get my hands on good stainless steel tanks for putting under my vans, but I stumbled across a real winner when I found out about the industrial Teflon-lined barrels now in use. These barrels can be found in 25 or 50 gallon sizes, and for a few dollars you have a rustproof first-class water or holding tank. Any industrial section of a large city will have scads of them around and some of the big buses will have enough room underneath to put the big 50 gallon jobs. I used heavy strap iron cradles to hold them and connected little electric pumps to them although I am about to replace this constant line pressure pump with a constant barrel pressure air pump which will use less to push a given amount of water. They are a little more trouble free as a bonus. We used some surplus transparent hose to hook up all the faucets. I have found that ordinary garden hose is too chintzy and rubber taints all the water that goes through it. Camper supply stores have a good cheap hose. I had given copper some thought but one good accidental freeze would have split it open and who can afford copper. I have insulated pipes and tanks but didn't on the bus in hopes a half-filled round tank wouldn't split and the very flexible clear stuff would give enough.

Generally speaking I have found that the more insulation one can get UNDER *er* rig the better. The sides and top should get insulated but often the factory insulation will suffice IF one puts a layer of something over the metal interior. Wood paneling does the job. Rubber-backed carpet glued down with contact cement is even better and regular carpet is better than nothing. Our bus bedroom is carpeted ceiling to floor in warm carpet that cost next to nothing because it was leftover material – large pieces would need cutting up anyway.

By far, the best thing to have on a floor is rubber backed commercial carpet although it is really hard to find at any reasonable price. Linoleum is okay if it isn't in squares, which soon loosen up. And long shag rug is totally impractical.

Some innovations that are very nice include a clear plastic or glass skylight and light proof window covers all around. The skylight can be incorporated into the ventilation cover if it is fairly large and the savings in lighting fuel will make the effort worthwhile. In cold weather this skylight should have a double layer of glass as well as the windows if possible, although a plastic film can be put on in a pinch.

Cold weather is really hard to combat in a bus or van and I always try to have sliding heavy curtains to cut off window areas and the front end driver window area from the more insulated section. After trying about everything I could think of to heat my various mobile shelters, I found the solution in the good ol' wood stove. The pressure and wick kerosene burners, the catalytic heaters, LP gas – they all have drawbacks for the full time "outbacker" or penny pincher. If at all possible give the LITTLE potbellied wood burner a chance – wherever you go, the fuel will probably be laying around waiting for you. A good armload will keep you snug all day and a little coal or hardwood will get you through the night. Even if daytime smoke will give you away where you are you can always stoke up after dark.

Get a good quality (will have a grate) stove with a five inch pipe and fix yourself a fairly heat-resistant and leakproof opening. The heat can be excessive at ceiling if a vent (preferably adjustable) is not available. If your rig is paneled at ceiling you will need a larger pipe to catch heat around the smaller five-inch pipe and carry it out so as not to scorch wood. Set the stove near and facing the door so you won't dribble splinters and ashes on your floor, and set it on a metal catch basin or scorch sheet. You can fix a carrier under your rig to hold your stovepipe when you are in cities and prefer to be less conspicuous. It is usually simple to put a choke (damper) in the pipe to adjust the flu draft and save wood. And add a screen spark arrestor. Ashley Stoves are the ticket for cabins and such, but the little flicker of flame required for a tight little van can be had from most any stick burner.

As far as name brand goes, keep in mind that you will probably wind up needing parts sooner or later and off-make vehicles can be a waste of all your loving labor if parts are scarce. Buses are really "bad news" when they start to have mechanical problems.

Dual wheels are desirable even though they need a little more gas to push them along – seems like I just keep collecting the exciting little goodies that civilization fosters and a single-wheeled rig I had got to the point of sinking down in warm parking lot asphalt pavement.

I believe in smaller engines but this is also derived from my penny-pinching approach which in turn comes from my dislike of sweating out my life for some members of the domination class.

Problems can occur with fire and I have parts gleaned from a rig that went up in flames from carelessness. Another friend lost a good converted van when he loaned it out to his good but insolvent friend. Provide for every emergency and take double precautions.

Still and all, considering the good and bad points, van and bus living is about the best money's worth of shelter to be had and, like adding rooms to a house, one can always get another one.

AUTO LIVING – IN A PINCH
By: John Freeman

While automobiles were not designed for spending any "sack out" time in, they certainly can do the job in a pinch. Over the years I have spent a lot of time living out of various cars & it certainly saved me a lot of funds that otherwise would have kept me longer at the distasteful working habit. I recall a 54 Chevy that had the steel bracing back of the rear seat removed with a little "keep the head level" padding & the seat out. The trunk & back seat area combined allowed plenty of room...Later I acquired a little Citroen 2-CV (18 HP) that had a rear seat that simply came out. I used this all over the West for a number of years. By removing the backing to the front seats, I & a mate had no trouble using the front seat area for the lower body.

I recall one memorable trip when I took a week's trip with 2 adults & 3 little kids in this tiny rig. With all the seats removed, it was like a bed, & even in the freezing weather it was more than warm from the body heat.

After being run off a Mexican beach a couple of years ago, I & a girl & 2 kids wound up in the town in this same rig. The beauty of this auto camping is that you usually attract no attention. I've spent years in various motor homes & buses & every once in a while I have gotten hassled in some strange town. I often overcome this by simply picking out a back street with a few houses on it & then explain what I'm doing to the persons in the home in back of where we park. People are always glad to aid a decent appearing nomad.

Once, while hitchhiking across the States in the dead of winter I managed to find enough small town auto back seats to survive in on my trek – yet I hate being cramped & curled up, & any car I own I alter enough to get a good nights sleep in. I'm not the only one. During a hard period in the '60s I recall several down on their $ & luck families who lived out of their converted cars in Mecca Canyon, a little haul east of Palm Springs.

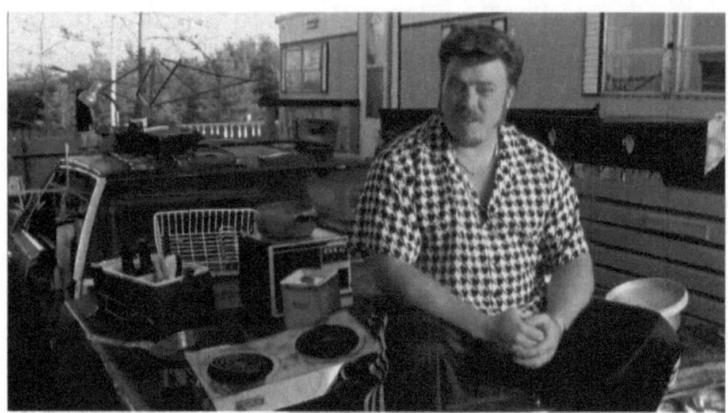

Ricky from the Trailer Park Boys frequently lives out of an old New Yorker.

At this place in time, most persons are too spoiled & warped in vacuum brained values to camp in cars. Yet to the true Vonuer, it's a great inconspicuous on the road shelter.

CONCLUDING LETTERS & NOTES

<u>NOTE FROM HAL S. (June 1987)</u>

I subscribed to VONU LIFE until it disappeared, & I always enjoyed it, though I felt it was mostly just wish fulfillment.

I have a small motorhome & spend 2 or 3 months a year out doing a lot of anonymous nothing. But I tend to stay in campgrounds, & as far as anyone's concerned, I'm just another vacationer.

I know people who live this way full time. It's less expensive & lots more fun than living in a house, but it's still not cheap.

There are <u>some</u> free (or nearly free) campgrounds in the US, but most of them are cluttered, crowded, and generally messy. You <u>can</u> sleep most of the night in highway rest areas, especially if you wait until after dark to park. Cops usually don't hassle you. I'm 68 years old & I think they're embarrassed to give me much trouble.

<u>LETTER FROM BRICK PILLOW (Dec. 1987)</u>

Jim, I was intrigued by Hal S.'s (too brief) remarks on motorhome living, in LIVING FREE 41. I've been living on the road, not in a fancy motorhome, but in my extremely basic truck, for almost ten months now. Heck, maybe the bludg in Washington are just so much sweeter than the rest of the country's, but I've never had any hassle at all about sleeping at the interstate rest areas. Not a once, and I've probably slept a hundred nights there. The badgers pull through once or twice a night, looking to break up beer parties 'n such, but if you're quietly eating, sleeping, cooking, reading, etc. they won't give you a second glance. I recommend rest areas – your highway taxes at work – to any weary light liver.

Road living, for those open-minded enough to consider it, is the easiest way I know how to break from the vicious circle of jobs, rents, taxes, and bills. For anyone who has a vehicle, the expense of living in it is hardly more than the expense of owning it.

All it took me to get started were some blankets, curtains for the windows (I'm using old towels, actually), a Coleman stove, ice chest, and some homemade bookshelves. For luxury, I bought myself one of those cigarette-lighter TVs, which was mostly a waste of money, because it never occurs to me to turn the darn thing on, so it mostly just sits.

That's as far as I've gotten fixing up the truck, but check with me again next summer, and see what I've done to it in that time. I figured I could spend five or ten more years on the treadmill dreaming, or I could start living the lazy life I wanted right away. The investment so far has been about $500 (I already had the truck), and the payoff has been well worth it: an exponential increase in peace of mind. There's plenty of freedoms available for anyone willing to put out a little effort.

Happy on the highway,
Brick

COMMENTS FOR BRICK PILLOW

What we have here is a difference between East and West. When I drove to Oregon & back in 1971, I found Interstate rest areas in the East heavily littered with signs reading: "No Overnight Parking." I assume it was enforced.

Since I meant to sleep in my car (1967 Toyota 4-door), my strategy was to get off the Interstate (I-80 most of the way), & make a quick search (30 minutes or so) to find a "squat-spot" suitable for an overnight stop. I did that all across the country & back, avoiding cities, looking for secluded rural area, that elusive dead-end dirt road with no one around, but usually settling for something rather more marginal.

My stops were: in Iowa, near Davenport; in the Nebraska panhandle, just outside Sidney; in Idaho, near Boise; & on the return trip: in Nevada, middle of the desert; in Wyoming, between the highway & Union Pacific railroad tracks which run parallel, parked next to an abandoned(?) railroad shed; in Nebraska, on non-descript farm roads criss-crossing through corn fields (poor spot); & in Indiana, in outer suburbs (very poor). An added difficulty was that during most of my trip, my headlights weren't working, so I couldn't drive until it was really pitch dark, as originally planned. That made it harder to slip into a spot unnoticed, but mandatory that I stop at dusk since I couldn't drive after dark. I managed okay.

THE END

Additional Resources

- **The Vonu Podcast**: If you want to learn more about anything covered in this book, I'd highly recommend you check out the podcast Kyle Rearden and I do. In season 1, we covered the philosophy of vonu, season 2 was the practice of vonu, and the current season, 3, is where we develop and update vonu to the modern day.
  - www.vonupodcast.com
- **Vonu: The Search for Personal Freedom, Number 2 – Letters from Rayo**
  - www.vonupodcast.com/vonu2
- **Vonulife, March 1973 (Special Edition)**
  - www.vonupodcast.com/vl
- **Ocean Freedom Notes**
  - www.vonupodcast.com/ofn
- **Self-Liberation Notes**
  - www.vonupodcast.com/sln
- **Going Mobile**
  - www.vonupodcast.com/gm
- **Low-Cost Living**
  - www.vonupodcast.com/lcl
- **Dwelling Portably [sic]**
  - www.vonupodcast.com/dp
- **Articles About Vonu**
  - www.vonupodcast.com/vonuarticles
- **Liberty Under Attack**: If you're seeking out paths to personal freedom, then you need to check out The Freedom Umbrella of Direct Action and the Direct Action Series.
  - www.libertyunderattack.com/FUDA
  - www.libertyunderattack.com/DAS
- **YouTube**: If you're pursuing any of the lifestyle changes or strategies covered above, then YouTube will be your best

friend. Recommended search terms: "van dwelling," "living aboard a boat," "minimalist sailboating," etc.

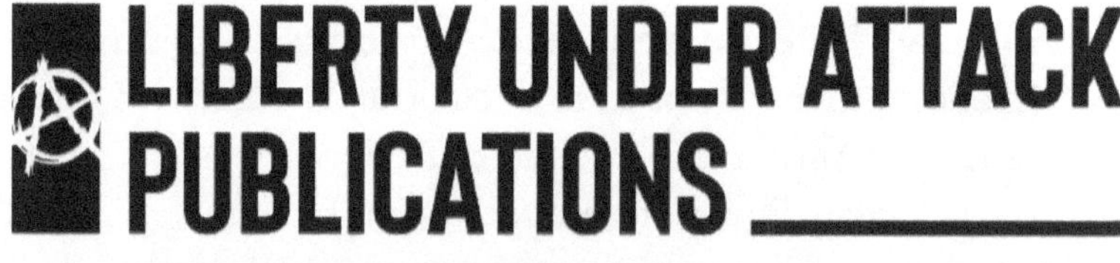

Support Us

If you enjoyed the book and found it valuable, please consider
shooting us some bitcoin!

Bitcoin: 15Bdzduwt92jYFGFaK2NSkPYFTaLbtonJg